PENNY STOCK TRADING

QuickStart Guide

SECOND EDITION

The Simplified Beginner's Guide To Penny Stock Trading

contents

BEFORE YOU START READING, DOWNLOAD YOUR FREE DIGITAL ASSETS!

Visit the URL below to access your free Digital Asset files that are included with the purchase of this book.

☑ Summaries
☑ Cheat Sheets
☑ Articles

☑ White Papers
☑ Charts & Graphs
☑ Reference Materials

DOWNLOAD YOURS HERE:

www.clydebankmedia.com/pennystocks-assets

Introduction

Penny stocks operate in a universe in which few things are certain, but the payoff potential is huge. They exist in a sparsely regulated, volatile section of the market, so consumers (investors) must always be on the lookout for frauds and hucksters. Nonetheless, gems are hidden within the chaos. If you're willing to do the research and take the risks, then you could realize substantial gains.

If you've elected to read this book, no doubt you're curious about the often confusing world of penny stocks. You don't want to lose your proverbial shirt, even though the word "penny" makes this investing venture seem less risky than most. In addition, penny stocks have gained a poor reputation in some investing circles, largely because it's easy to make mistakes when you're choosing where to invest.

We've designed this quick start guide to help you avoid the most common mistakes beginning penny stock investors make and to teach you specifics such as proper trading strategies, how to trade risk-free, and – most of all – how to spot those companies that will grow and add to your profits. It's a great feeling when you succeed, especially when you can watch your small investment grow to something more substantial.

| 1 |

Stocks 101

Perhaps you're brand new to the world of investing. Maybe you've chosen to read this guide because penny stocks seemed like a fairly inexpensive way to stick your toe in the investment waters, so to speak. But how much do you really know about the *stock market* in general?

We tend to throw around the terms "stock" and "stock market" quite freely, but do you really know what these two terms mean? Perhaps you learned about them in a college or high school economics class, or maybe your parents invested in the stock market and you remember hearing them talk about their gains and losses. However, it's important that the details in your head be a little more complete before you go stampeding into the penny stock world.

What is a Stock?

Quite simply put, a *stock* is a piece of a company, albeit a very small piece in most cases. When a company chooses to be a "public" company, it issues shares of stock for purchase by the general public. The more "stocks" or pieces you purchase, the more of the company you own.

As one of the co-owners of the company, often along with thousands or even millions of others, you are entitled to a portion of that company's profits. If the company does well, your stock goes up in price and you make money. You may reap this money in the form of dividends, which are sums of money paid out to investors on a regular basis (usually quarterly).

Note : some companies do not pay dividends, even when they are doing well, preferring to reinvest the profits back into the business in order to earn more in the future with the promise of even higher dividends ahead.

If the company in which you are investing experiences losses, you take a loss on your investment, too. In this case, the dividends you receive are lower or, in some cases, you don't receive any at all.

This is why you may hear about the *risk* involved in "playing the stock market". Even investing in reputable companies represents a risk if something happens to affect the company negatively. It's often a guessing game, as you'll see later, when we begin to discuss penny stocks. This is why investing in the stock market is often referred to as "speculation", a word that literally means "forming a theory without firm evidence."

Types of Stock

There are two basic types of stock – common and preferred.

1. Common Stock

Most often offered to the general public. When you buy common shares of stock, you own a piece of the company and are entitled to dividends – or a piece of the profit. For each share you own, you get one vote in the election that determines board members, who are the individuals who oversee any decisions made by management. Common stock can be a very good investment but does indeed carry risk due to bankruptcies, liquidations, mergers, etc.

2. Preferred Stocks

Generally provide investors with a fixed dividend for as long as you own the stock. This is unlike common stocks, for which the dividends undoubtedly vary. If a company liquidates, preferred stockholders are paid off before common stock holders, which presents an obvious advantage. However, preferred stock holders usually do not have the same voting rights as common stock holders.

Why Do Companies Sell Stock?

A company sells stock when it needs to raise money. It can also do this by borrowing funds from a bank or other source. However, if its owners choose to sell stock, there are no repayment plans to be faced in the future.

There are a few different ways to sell stock. If a company's owners want to control who is offered a piece of the pie, they sell stock through "private placement", which allows management to choose to whom the stock is offered. Chances are that if you've purchased stock or plan to do so in the future, you've done so through a public offering. Companies initiate public offerings, as was noted, in order to raise money. They may need money for a variety of reasons, including expansion or any other kind of further growth, or to pay back owners or investors who had a hand in getting the company started.

Companies institute an initial public offering (IPO), which is the first offering of stock, but can also continue later with a secondary public offering if they need to raise more capital.

A company whose stock is performing well is usually considered a solid company and tends to have an easier time raising money through lenders as well, besides through the sale of stock.

The Stock Market

The Stock Market is the place where stocks and bonds are "traded" (bought and sold). Simply put, a stock market links buyers and sellers, facilitating the exchange of securities between these two groups of investors.

A Stock Market can be a physical place where face-to-face trading happens, such as the big Stock Exchange in New York City, or more likely a "virtual" location, a network where trades are made electronically.

There are two parts to the Stock Market.

1. The Primary Market

Where new issues of stock are sold through the aforementioned Initial Public Offerings or IPOs. Institutional Investors – those who have extremely large dollar amounts to spend – use the primary markets to purchase shares at Initial Public Offerings and are given preferential treatment due to the dollar amount they plan to purchase.

2. The Secondary Market

Where "the little guy" makes his or her purchases. After the IPO, all subsequent trading happens on the secondary market, with offerings now available to individual purchasers like you.

The two largest stock exchanges in the world are the New York Stock Exchange, which was founded way back in 1792, and the NASDAQ, which was founded in 1971. These days, most trading happens electronically, and stocks are held in electronic form. In the "old days", stocks were issued as physical certificates, which stated how many shares you owned.

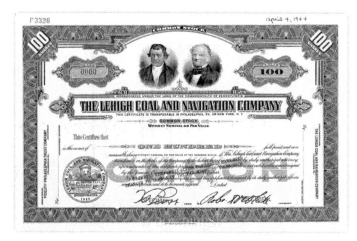

Fg. 1 : An example of a paper certificate used to certify stock ownership.

| 2 |

Penny Stock Basics

A *penny stock* is a stock that trades for less than $5 per share. This threshold is the easiest, though perhaps not the most precise, method by which to identify a penny stock. But, much like other factors in the penny stock market, this definition is very much in flux. Some experts say that $1 per share is a more appropriate threshold, but penny stocks can trade for as little as – appropriately – one cent.

Market capitalization value (market cap) also enters into the equation when defining a penny stock. Market cap refers to the total value of shares multiplied by the total number of outstanding shares. Some say that when a company's market cap value is less than 10 million, its stocks appropriately qualify as "penny stocks." Others say the market cap threshold is closer to 25 million, and others say 100 million or even more.

As you can see, these definitions are a bit fly-by-night, a reflection of this security's widely unregulated, unstandardized status. Definitional difficulties were among the problems that needed to be addressed as governments, such as the State of Georgia, attempted to specifically regulate penny stocks.

The Georgia Law

In 1990, decorated Vietnam veteran and future Georgia Senator, Max Cleland, then Georgia Secretary of State, drafted legislation to protect consumers from being defrauded by brokerages that dealt in penny stocks.[1] It was observed that the value of penny stocks

---

[1] http://articles.latimes.com/1990-03-20/business/fi-532_1_penny-stock

could be manipulated much more easily than could the value of standard, exchange-traded stocks. Brokers took advantage, using the impressionability of these stocks to defraud investors into making big expensive trades, while they, the brokers, took as much as 50% of the trade value as commission. In other words, if an investor could sell $5,000 worth of low-cost volatile stock, then the broker could make as much as $2,500 on a single transaction, just for the sale. Even if the investor lost all of his money, the broker would still keep his commission.

This commission-driven approach by brokers to exploit penny stocks was depicted in Martin Scorsese's 2013 Jordan Belfort bio-epic, *The Wolf of Wall Street*. In the film, Belfort is seen telephone pitching the story of a fly-by-night penny stock company to a naïve investor.[2] Unlike a wise (or moral) penny stock broker, Belfort knows very little about the company he's pitching. All he cares about is collecting a whopping 50% commission off of the sale. He convinces the investor to buy several thousand dollars of a bad penny stock and laughs all the way to the bank.

In part, Max Cleland's 1990 legislation prevented brokers from collecting any more than a 10% commission on the trade of penny stocks. Brokers had previously been able to corrupt penny stocks so thoroughly because penny stocks did not—and still do not—trade on the big public exchanges. They trade on what are known as **over-the-counter (OTC) exchanges**. OTC exchanges refer to any stock trading network that operates outside the formal, publicly accessible exchanges, such as the New York Stock Exchange (NYSE), Toronto Stock Exchange (TSX), and the Tokyo Stock Exchange (TSE). It's through the use of the OTC exchanges that crooked investors are able to get away with charging exorbitant commissions. Since there's no widely-public ledger confirming the true price of the penny stock, the investor

---

[2] Scorsese, Martin, dir. The Wolf of Wall Street. Paramount, 2013.

can easily charge $1.50 per share for a stock that he or she purchased for $1.00 per share.

One of the additional provisions in the 1990 Georgia law requires brokers to create a paper record (a written agreement along with a risk disclosure document) that discloses, among other things, the amount the investor paid for the stock. Investors can verify that they are buying the stock at a price very close to what the company (not the broker) is selling it for, and that the brokers take only the standard 10 percent for their commissions.

The law passed in Georgia was challenged and upheld in federal court,[3] eventually becoming the template for several other states seeking to regulate the trade of penny stocks. Soon thereafter, the US Securities and Exchange Commission (SEC) updated its regulatory scheme on penny stocks.

The general consensus is that, while brokers have to go through more hoops to profit from buying and selling penny stocks, there are still significant fraud risks, most notably the ***pump and dump*** scheme, which is discussed in Chapter 7.

The Low Down on Over-the-Counter (OTC) Markets

The key thing to remember about OTC markets is that the stocks that are traded on these markets, unlike those traded on the public exchanges, are not subject to minimum standard requirements in order to be sold on the exchange. Take for instance the New York Stock Exchange (NYSE). In order for a company to be featured on the New York Stock Exchange, it has to be profitable and it has to have generated a certain amount of revenue, which can be verified over the last several years.

---

[3] http://www.deseretnews.com/article/111783/GEORGIA-LAW-WONT-HURT-BROKERS-JUDGE-RULES.html?pg=all

In other words, to be featured on the NYSE, the company must possess some critical features of a "healthy" company, a company that has real market value. Companies that trade in OTC markets don't necessarily have to have any cash coming in or any profit recorded. Many of these companies may have unpredictable and undocumented earnings records. Their management may be incredibly inexperienced, unqualified, or even disinterested. The products and services these companies offer may be in areas of the market that are as yet untested.

Not all OTC markets are created equal. In fact, as an expert penny stock investor, you must learn how to discern quality exchanges from suspect exchanges. Chapter 2 of this book reviews how to find a good exchange.

Fig. 2

Over the Counter (OTC) Markets	VS.	Traditional Public Exchanges (NYSE, NASDAQ etc.)
❌	stock-issuing companies must have turned a profit	✅
❌	trades are supervised by a central mediating authority	✅
✅	stock prices can easily be manipulated	❌
❌	reliable liquidity	✅
❌	listed companies must file financial reports with the SEC	✅

Can I Make Money With Penny Stocks?

You've probably purchased this book because you're interested in making profitable investments. You've heard stories of outrageous returns, and you're comfortable using small amounts of money to make exceptionally aggressive investments. Well, in order to make money with penny stocks, you're going to have to do some research. Picking penny stocks from an OTC market *at random* is a very easy and efficient way to throw away your money.

Instead, this book will help you to identify certain characteristics of penny stocks that make them more likely to be big winners. Yes, you can definitely make money by investing in penny stocks. Ford Motor Co. was once a penny stock, so was American Airlines. Monster Beverage, makers of the famous Monster energy drink was once a penny stock, trading at 69 cents per share in 1995, now trading at a 52-week high of $70.49 per share.[4] That's a 10,000 percent growth rate! Obviously, the road from penny stock to blue chip does exist, even if it's sparsely traveled. That doesn't mean you can't get in the car and drive it, if you do your due diligence.

What a Penny Stock Investor Looks Like

Penny stocks are clearly not for everyone. Many investors prefer safer investments that are likely to grow steadily over long periods of time and have almost no chance of going belly up. The penny stock investor is cut from a slightly different cloth. If you're wondering whether or not you're a penny stock investor in your heart of hearts, then consider the following factors.

- *Do you enjoy actively managing and monitoring your portfolio?*
The typical medium-to-large cap investor (someone who buys stocks in larger companies) doesn't really need to spend too much time researching her investments and monitoring their day-to-day performance. Maybe once a quarter she'll make some trades and evaluate how her stocks have performed, but it won't be a

---

[4] http://www.benzinga.com/trading-ideas/long-ideas/14/01/3014935/9-one-time-penny-stocks-didnt-stay-that-way

particularly heady endeavor. The successful penny stock investor, by contrast, actively monitors and manages her portfolio. She knows that even if a penny stock looks good one week, a few factors can shuffle around quite quickly, and the stock will look like a disaster the next week. She'll want to get out before it's too late. This type of active monitoring and frequent buying and selling requires time but also money, as you'll presumably be paying more commission for more frequent trading.

- *Will you be satisfied with a modest return?*

It's important to set up reasonable expectations for your penny stock investment. Since there's so much hype behind penny stocks, many new investors expect big returns right out of the gate. The odds that you're just going to stumble upon a big winner are incredibly low. If you're smart and diligent, then you have a decent chance of seeing some modest growth in the value of your portfolio over time. If you're going into penny stocks with the expectation that you're going to get rich quickly, then you are setting yourself up for disappointment.

- *Can you tell when someone's lying to you?*

A good penny stock investor needs to have a good BS detector, because a lot of BS gets flung around in this space. Get ready to confront and size up a lot of over-hyped reviews about how 'Company A or Company B is poised to change the world' and the like. Stories are important, but you should never make an investment based on a story alone. You're going to need to see important financial metrics, such as *price-to-book*, *price-to-sales*, and other important measurements that allow you to size up the company's true potential. This book discusses these and other metrics in the subsequent chapters. But for now, just know that you can't be gullible if you want to succeed as a penny stock investor.

- ### *Do you cope well with risk?*

If you're delving into penny stocks, then you need to accept that there is a certain amount of risk. You may wind up watching your investments go up in smoke left and right, but you may also watch them multiply aggressively. If you flinch at risk and prefer securities that are more, well, "secure," then penny stocks may not be for you. As a good rule of thumb, you should only go into penny stocks if you have enough disposable income to support your investments. If you're taking money out of crucial household budgets—rent, food, car payment— just to buy more penny stocks, then you're acting irresponsibly.

- ### *Are you ok with letting it ride?*

Unlike larger securities, penny stocks are not so easily liquidated. For common stocks, you can usually buy or sell on any day that the market is open. Penny stock investors don't enjoy the same level of liquidity. You may find yourself in the incredibly frustrating position of watching your stock rise aggressively but being unable to sell it before it dips back down again. It comes with the territory.

Investing vs. Trading: The Difference

Most individuals who dabble in the stock market, including brokers and stock experts, pretty much use the terms investing and trading interchangeably, inferring that the two are synonymous with one another. However, those well-versed in penny stocks indicate that they are two markedly different things with different risks, different time commitments, and certainly diverse results.

Investing in penny stocks – without doing lots of constant trading – requires an individual with plenty of patience. Investors tend to "let it ride" rather than cashing out for small gains. The investor is the researcher and the wearer of rose-colored glasses. He's in it for the duration and, as such, stands to make larger gains than the trader.

Investing is wise in the penny stock market, especially for those new to the realm. But while it tends it be easier than being a trader, that doesn't mean there isn't work involved. The work tends to be more up-front at the beginning of the investment process. For example, an investor needs to jump into the often tedious task of investigating the penny stock companies in which he wishes to invest. This involves making calls, pouring over figures, and putting it all together to make wise purchasing decisions. This takes time to do correctly, but the result is generally a better feeling about the stock purchased. Potentially, there may be less risk involved as well.

Investors stand to recognize more gains than traders because they tend to keep shares for a longer amount of time and, hence, they see prices rise over and over again rather than jumping to cash in at the first or second gain, fearing that it might be their only chance. Most experts note that investing really is the best approach in the penny stock market.

> *"With investing, you can get involved with small companies before or as they get discovered and ride the share prices dramatically higher for gains of 2 times, 5 times, or even 20 times your money,"* explains Peter Leeds, who has penned numerous investing books. *"A trader generally takes her profits at much lower levels..."* [5]

While the investor is the painter content to hone his masterpiece a few strokes at a time over several months, the trader is the child who spends his money as soon as he gets it without waiting to amass a considerable sum with which he could buy something much bigger... if only he had the patience. But, for him, those small rewards are much more exciting.

---

[5] Leeds, Peter. "Chap. 5: Developing a Strategy." *Penny Stocks for Dummies.* Hoboken: John Wiley & Sons, 2013. 90-91. Print.

Traders are in it for the short-term gains and is discontent with the idea of "wait and see". They are impatient players who rarely take the time to thoroughly research each penny stock company, as do investors. So, they depend mostly on the information available on trading charts to make their decisions about which shares to buy and which to by-pass.

You might think that takes less work. Well, it certainly does... at the beginning of the process. *Trading* demands a much more active role in the health of one's stock portfolio. Because traders are only looking to make these short-term gains, they spend much more time buying and selling. They may even buy and sell several times in a day or dozens of times in a week. For them, it's a nail-biting process they enjoy, which allows for perhaps a 10 or 20 percent gain each time, small tidbits that are less likely to result in significant profits, even over the long stretch. Nonetheless, it's a game that keeps the adrenaline pumping.

Again, investing is the better strategy for the novice, especially one who has entered the market with some trepidation, but trading – with all of its excitement – seems to be best suited for those with a considerable amount of stock market know-how, even if that know-how hasn't been developed in the world of penny stocks.

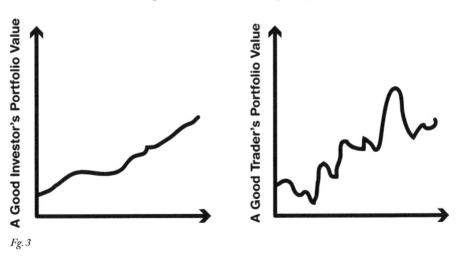

Fg. 3

| 3 |
Not All Markets Are Created Equal

Many nominal "penny stocks" – if we define a penny stock to be any stock trading at $5 or less – can be found on the major stock exchanges. And while investors may enjoy a degree of assurance that any NYSE stock is a legitimate stock representing a legitimate company, the NYSE listing alone doesn't make that company a good investment. In fact, going after stocks on any market purely on the basis of their being "cheap" is not a well-thought-out investment strategy.

If you find a penny stock on a major exchange that's under $5, what you're usually looking at is a company that's had a severe downturn and is not in good health. The infamous National Bank of Greece and the troubled drug store, Rite Aid, are examples of stocks that are currently trading for less than $5 per share.[6] It's important to understand that even though you may still see Rite Aid as a big, national drug company and the Bank of Greece as an historically eminent institution, there is *no* guarantee or evidence whatsoever that these companies will ever gain back the value that they once possessed. They could file for bankruptcy, they could dissolve, or they could retain their current (or close to their current) valuation for decades on end. The lesson here is: cheap does not equal hot. If they're cheap, then they're probably cheap for a reason. And if you're dealing with a well-respected market like the NYSE, then you can assume that the "reasons" are somewhat "reasonable." Once you begin looking at cheap stocks in less regulated, less accessible, and less liquid markets, you have to deal with an even greater degree of uncertainty while being even more scrupulous about your choices.

---

[6] http://www.marketwatch.com/story/buying-cheap-stocks-is-an-expensive-mistake-2013-09-26

The exchange on which a penny stock trades is your first clue as to whether or not it's a wise investment.[7] You should be able to find the name of the exchange on your brokerage site (where you actually buy and sell stock) or on a market analytics site such as *OTCMarkets.com*, where the exchanges are tiered into OTCQX ("the best marketplace"), OTCQB ("the venture marketplace"), and OTC Pink ("the open marketplace"). The site publishes a list of criteria that define the reporting requirements for each market, with OTC Pink clearly being the least regulated, though even OTC Pink has a minimum quality threshold that, if violated, requires that a special marker be placed next to each listing that may be exceptionally problematic. Upon inspecting some of the tens of thousands of companies featured on these OTC exchanges, it is apparent that the most abundant collection of penny stocks are found on OTC Pink, though they may also be found on OTCQB, and OTCQX. As was previously mentioned, penny stocks are also not precluded from being offered on the big exchanges, such as the NYSE. When dealing with penny stocks, it's all about getting as much information as you can about the stock you wish to buy, and the market on which the stock is traded is an important source of insight. Here's why:

Exchanges don't seek out the companies they list. The companies must do the legwork of researching and deciding where they want to be listed (and where they can feasibly qualify to be listed). There's a *huge* differential in requirement between getting your company listed on the pink sheets (or OTC Pink) and getting your company listed in the New York Stock Exchange. To be listed in the pink sheets, or on OTC Pink, a company need only file a single piece of unaudited paperwork, a "Form 211." The Form 211 is filed with *FINRA* (the Financial Industry Regulatory Authority). The company must then find a *market maker*. A market maker is a broker-dealer who is willing to buy some stock from

---

[7] Leeds, Peter. Penny Stocks for Dummies. Hoboken, NJ, John Wiley and Sons, Inc. 2013.

the company so that they can turn around and sell it for a profit. Once a broker-dealer is approached with information about a company, they quote a price and then purchase a quantity of stock for resale.

It's important to note here that the broker-lender is investing in a stock only for the purpose of trading the stock away. What's most important for the broker-lender is not how well the stock does, but how well it sells. This is why broker-traders are willing to bring in stocks from the pink sheets with very little information attached. Many of these companies do not even file their financial reports with the SEC, which can make it very difficult to research them in any depth.

As in individual investor open to buying penny stocks, you must accept that many of the penny stock listings that come from the pink sheets, OTC Pink, or other sparsely regulated markets, leave you with very minimal information about the companies in which you're investing. Many penny stocks are thus doomed to be nothing more than a name and a price quote. Buyer be warned: these stocks are a pure gamble. On the flip side, if you find a penny stock trading on the pink sheets or OTC Pink that *is* reporting annually or periodically to the SEC, then perhaps you've stumbled upon a serious company. Combine these factors with a few others and you've got a viable prospect.

Understanding the variations between exchanges will help you understand the positioning and objectives of the companies that these exchanges feature. Companies seek a listing on an exchange not as a matter of legal compliance or public accounting, but because it *benefits* them to do so. Companies pay fees to be listed on certain exchanges, such as the NYSE, which can run upwards of $100,000 just to list. When considering investment in a penny stock, it's helpful to find out how much the company is laying out in order to be featured on the exchange in which they're being traded. In addition to fees, exchanges may have various ongoing reporting requirements for their member companies. Failure to abide by these requirements could result in the removal of the company from the exchange.

Some exchanges mandate that a corporation have a board of directors listed. As you can imagine, many investors want to know who's running these companies. Do they have solid business track records and the right experience? Now, let's say that you were able to find out information about a company's board of directors even though the exchange on which that company's stock is trading does not require a disclosure of the board members. At this point you would need to ask yourself why the company chose an exchange without this requirement. Perhaps they didn't want investors to know about a particular person's involvement in the company, or maybe it was because they just didn't want to spend the extra fees necessary to be featured in a more prominent exchange. Either of these factors could prove useful in your buying or selling decision. When you get information about a company's board of directors, you're getting information about the people who will be making decisions on your behalf. The board often controls the hiring and firing of executives, executive salaries, and the issuing of dividends to stockholders, among other things.

Some exchanges also protect investors by requiring publicly-traded companies to work with an investor relations firm or some other designated party who is responsible for answering questions about the company. Having a good investor relations contact at the ready, especially when dealing with penny stocks, is invaluable.

Companies may also wish to be traded in markets alongside other companies similar to their own. This way, if an investor is looking to invest in tech stocks, he'll go to a certain exchange—in the case of tech stocks, the NASDAQ—to look over the offerings. The market in which a company chooses to be traded reflects what that company truly is at heart, or at least what it thinks it is at the moment. Companies are under no obligation to remain on one exchange indefinitely, but may bring their stocks to different exchanges as they expand or shrink.

When it comes to choosing the right market, a company is always looking to balance the costs and the benefits. If you can spot a company moving from a weaker exchange (fewer barriers to entry) to a stronger one, then there may be a story there. Company X may be looking for investment from a new crowd. It may have developed better financial reporting. Get as much information about the company as you can and see if its recent venue switch offers a compelling reason to invest.

To Recap

- Among the over-the-counter markets, OTCQX and OTCQB require stricter financial standards than OTC Pink. Companies listed in OTCQX must comply with US Securities laws.

  Note : You will also likely come across stocks listed in the OTCBB exchange, "Over-the-Counter Bulletin Board." The NASDAQ owns and operates the OTCBB, and like the OTCQX, OTCBB stocks are subject to SEC oversight.

- If you find a penny stock (trading at under $5) on an established market like the NYSE, be sure to investigate the company's back-story, as you are usually dealing with a very troubled security.

- When stocks are featured only on the pink sheet, OTC Pink, or other barely regulated markets, do not invest in them unless you have substantial knowledge about the company from outside sources. To do so would be nothing short of a pure gamble, with odds that aren't in your favor.

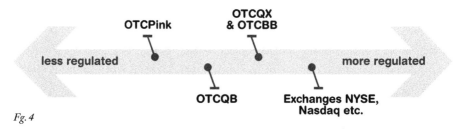

Fg. 4

| 4 |

A Few Key Investing Metrics

This chapter reviews some critical metrics to help you make better decisions when choosing penny stocks. Every good investment is essentially built on a story, a reason why the current price for a particular security is lower than it should be. Even though you can't predict the future, the ability to tell a compelling story that forecasts a probable future outcome can be a powerful tool. But, since you're dealing with dollars and cents, profits and loss, you need to incorporate rock hard data into your stories wherever possible.

Penny stocks usually draw a lot of attention from investors because they're cheap to acquire. Investors who only have a few hundred dollars to throw into the market are drawn to penny stocks because they can buy a substantial quantity, and, at times, realize astronomical gains. You're reading this book because you want to maximize your chances at realizing a great return. You want to do more than just shoot from the hip and hope something sticks. You want strategy.

Liquidity Ratios

Understanding how to use *liquidity ratios* insulates you from one of the major hazards of penny stock investing—investing in a company that cannot pay its short-term obligations. Many stocks are priced low specifically because they are unable to service their debts. You want to steer clear of these stocks, and you can easily do so by learning how to access and interpret these relatively simple ratios. What's more, beginning your due diligence with an assessment of liquidity ratios sets you up to find companies that are in a strong position, capable of servicing their debts and, hopefully, growing their business.

Here's what you need to know:

Current Ratio

The **Current Ratio** liquidity ratio is found by dividing a company's current assets by its current liabilities.

Fg. 5

$$\text{current ratio} = \frac{\text{current assets}}{\text{current liabilities}}$$

You're looking for a value of 1 or higher, indicating that the company has enough value in its assets to cover its currently outstanding liabilities. If the ratio is 1/3, then you want to stay away from this penny stock. Its debt is three times as large as the value of its current assets. If the ratio, on the other hand, has a value of 3, then you know that the company's assets are sufficient to cover its liabilities three times over.

Quick Ratio

The **quick ratio** is essentially the current ratio but with more restrictions placed upon what qualifies as an "asset." The quick ratio defines assets as only cash, accounts receivable, and marketable securities.

Note : Marketable securities include stocks, bonds, and guaranteed investment certificates due to mature in the next 12 months.

The objective of the quick ratio is to give the investor a sense for the value of a company's assets that can be quickly and expediently liquidated. The quick ratio is thought to be more accurate than the current ratio as well, seeing as some of the assets included in the current ratio may not be truly liquid and may not have the same value when resold. Like the current ratio, the investor should seek a value of 1 or higher to feel at ease with the company's ability to service its short-term debts.

Cash Ratio

Cash is king, and a good *cash ratio* makes a penny stock investment even safer than just a good quick ratio. The cash ratio is essentially the quick ratio with accounts receivable removed from the calculation. You're left with cash plus marketable securities divided by liabilities. By removing accounts receivable, you no longer need to worry about whether the company's customers are ever going to pay them. Everything they have immediately on-hand is accounted for and nothing else. With penny stocks, it's not necessarily a deal breaker if a company has a weaker cash ratio. A value of at least 1 is a good benchmark to ensure that the company will be able to remain in business and service all of its debts due within the next 12 months.

Operating Cash Flow Ratio

Operating cash flow is an even stricter measurement of a company's short-term financial solvency. This liquidity ratio is calculated using only the incoming cash from company operations in the numerator and dividing it by the company's current liabilities.

Fg. 6

$$\text{operational cash flow ratio} = \frac{\text{incoming cash from operations}}{\text{current liabilities}}$$

In the case of this ratio, it's ok if your value is less than 1, as other liquid assets can be brought in if needed to service the company's debts, but if the *operating cash flow ratio* drops too low, then the company may be facing some serious financial trouble. If the operating cash flow is 1 or more, then the company is bringing in enough cash through normal business operations to service its debts for the next 12 months, which is a really good sign for a penny stock.

Note : As a general rule, investors like companies that have solid cash flow and the ability to readily cover all of their debts. If you can find a company in this position priced cheaply (see Price-to-Book, Price-to-Earnings, an Price-to-Sales below), then you've found a good penny stock prospect.

There are several reasons why a stock's operating cash flow is important:

- If the company has a strong operating cash flow, then it must be bringing in a substantial income, meaning whatever products or services are being sold are reaching a significant market, and that market is likely to continue creating a real demand.

- When operational cash flow is heavy, the company is in a position to take advantage of growth opportunities. The company may hire new employees, invest in new assets, or purchase back its own stock shares.

- A company with a strong operational cash flow is less likely to take on more debt. Without the need to raise more money slowing it down, the company is free to focus on further expansions of its business.

Ratio Components : The Basics

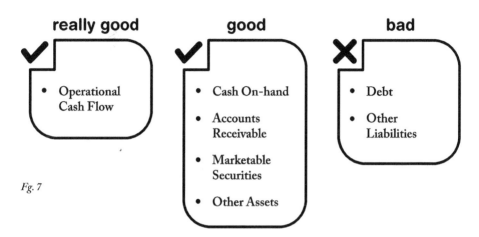

Fg. 7

Price-to-Book

The price-to-book ratio, or P/B ratio, is an interesting indicator that can help you determine whether a stock, regardless of its share price, is actually "cheap." Let's take a fictional penny stock, Brayton Co., or "BYT," that trades for $3. Let's say that BYT is listed on the OTCQX, so you've got access to some decent financial data. To find the stock's P/B ratio, you first need to get its market capitalization (market cap) value, which, on the QTCQX is listed next to every stock. Market cap simply refers to the number of outstanding shares multiplied by the share value. Let's say BYT has 3 million outstanding shares and thus has a market cap of $9 million. Next, you need to find the company's ***book price***. A company's book price is what the company would be left with after all of its assets were liquidated and all of its liabilities paid. A company's book price can usually be determined by looking at its most recent balance sheet—a listing of all assets and liabilities. Now let's say that you are able to find BYT's book price and that the company "goes to book" at 12 million dollars. This means that the company is selling at three quarters of its book value (below book value), which is another way of saying it's "cheap" or perhaps a good deal.

Fg. 8

$$\text{price to book} \atop \text{(p/b) ratio} = \frac{\text{market cap}}{\text{book price}} \text{ or } \frac{\text{share price}}{\text{per share book value}}$$

> *Note : Sometimes P/B ratio is calculated using all per share values. The company's book value per share would be determined. In our example, BYT would have a per share book value of 12 million divided by 3 million, or a book value per share of $4. The P/B ratio would thus be 3/4. You will always get the same P/B value, no matter which calculation method you use. Some investors like to look at per share book value and compare it to the stock value.*

In theory, the P/B ratio is exceptionally important for penny stocks because the companies that issue penny stocks are more likely to be on the brink of bankruptcy. If a company's share value is lower than its per share book value, and the company goes bankrupt immediately, then theoretically the loss would be smaller than it would have been had the share value been higher than the book value. Therefore, investing in companies with a lower P/B ratio can serve as a stop-loss against risky investments.

As with any financial ratio investors use, a company's price-to-book can bode both well and poorly for the company's future stock value. In our example, BYT's stock is selling for less than its per share book value. Some investors would say that this is an indication that the stock has been under-priced, and, assuming that the company is still fundamentally in good shape and there aren't any unpleasant surprises, the stock should go up in value. So get in now! While it's hot! Another investor may look at the stock and think: it's a penny stock; it's likely to go bankrupt, best case the investors get some of their money back and take a modest loss. Not so good.

It's important to realize here that a strategy is not following a fail-safe, inflexible plan of operation, but building a knowledge base in order to make informed decisions. This is the classic difference between "strategy" and "tactics." Tactics refer to a clear-cut action plan that, if executed correctly, produces a very specific result. Strategy refers to the more artistic pursuit of gently honing the larger picture toward your vision for success. When it comes to investments, calculating a penny stock's P/B ratio is a tactic, and deciding whether or not to buy the stock is a strategy.

Growth Rates

Anyone can easily understand this metric. What does the penny stock's growth history look like? Has the stock been taking a steady plummet over the last several quarters, or is it ascending to great heights with no end in sight?

When assessing a stock's growth pattern, make sure that you're looking at quarterly markers, if not monthly. Looking at a stock's growth on a year-by-year basis can be a bit deceptive, as smaller yet meaningful growth changes can occur within the confines of a year. If you only look at growth benchmarks on a year-by-year basis, then you may miss crucial patterns.

Take, for example, a stock that has a market cap value of $25M in the spring quarter of 2014. It grows to 40M in the summer quarter, then begins declining to $35M in the fall quarter and is at 33M in the winter quarter. In the spring quarter of 2015, it's at $30M. The market cap value has declined over the last three quarters. And, so long as you're evaluating the stock in quarterly increments, you will see this. If an investor fails to review the quarterly increments and only evaluates the stock in annual increments, seeing Spring 2014 at $25M and then Spring 2015 at $30M, he may mistakenly think that the stock is on a steady upward trajectory.

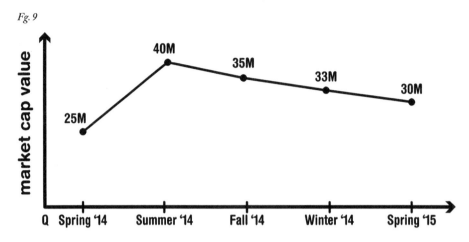

Fg. 9

The same mistaken evaluation can occur in the inverse: the stock has a market cap value of $30M in the spring of 2014. It slumps to $15M by the summer of 2014, it's at $20M and $23M, in the fall and winter quarters. By spring of 2015 the stock continues its steady ascent to $26M, but, if the investor were looking at the stock on a year-by-year basis, then she would see that it was at $30M in the spring of 2014 and $26M in the spring of 2015. She may thus assume that the growing stock is actually stagnant.

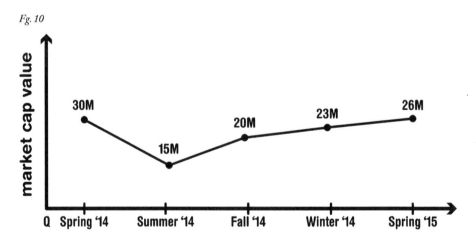

Fg. 10

So what really makes a stock go up in value? The simple answer to that question is market demand. If more people are willing to pay more money for the stock, then the stock price ascends. It's commonly thought that higher sales and higher revenue are directly proportional to stock price. This is not necessarily true. Companies don't necessarily have to be growing in sales for the stocks to go up, but such growth is one of the signs that may demarcate a big winner.

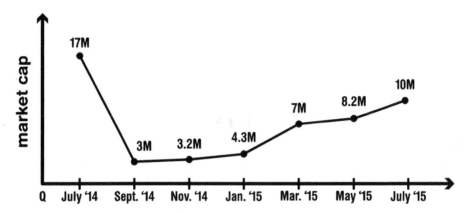

Fg. 11 : The graph above depicts another example of how the unique volatility of Penny Stocks can mislead annual trends.

The Price-to-Earnings Ratio

The "P/E" ratio allows you to evaluate how hot your penny stock is, at least in terms of its current ability to generate earnings. You have to be a bit wary here with penny stocks, as they can be seriously overvalued.[8] To define the price-to-earnings ratio, divide the company's market cap by its earnings for the most recent year. You may also define the ratio by dividing the share price of the stock by the stock's revenue per share.

Fg. 12

$$\text{price to earnings (p/e) ratio} = \frac{\text{market cap}}{\text{total earnings}} \text{ or } \frac{\text{share price}}{\text{earnings per share}}$$

---

[8] http://www.investopedia.com/articles/investing/061915/most-crucial-financial-ratios-penny-stocks.asp#ixzz3oYvip8D8

Let's go back to our example stock, Brayton Co. (BYT), which trades for $3 and has a market cap of $9M. Now let's say that BYT's earnings for the past year was $6M. BYT's price-to-earnings ratio is 9/6 or 3/2. If you want to calculate its price-to-earnings ratio using earnings per share as the denominator, you simply divide the total revenue ($6M) by the total number of outstanding shares, 3M, and you have your earnings per share -- $2. BYT share price ($3) over earnings per share ($2) = 3/2.

Usually what you're looking for, as an investor, is a company that has a low price-to-earnings ratio. You want the company's per share earnings to outstrip its per share cost. The only assumption you have to make is that more earnings leads to opportunities for more growth, and, of course, more growth means a higher stock valuation. A low price-to-earnings ratio could be another indicator that the stock is "cheap," a good deal. In the case of BYT, it looks like its stock price is higher than its per share earnings, perhaps because its price-to-book ratio is favorable. Maybe investors don't see an amazing growth opportunity but are willing to pay slightly more for the stock because its P/B ratio tells them its assets are intrinsically valuable.

Hopefully, you are beginning to see how various metrics connect with one another and can, in tandem, influence a stock's price along with its estimated growth potential. With penny stocks, the investor is faced simultaneously with advantage and disadvantage. The advantage is that with good research and attention to key metrics, it's easier to spot promising penny stock investment opportunities because penny stocks are more volatile in general. You're more likely to stumble upon a stock that's both "cheap" and seems to have good growth potential. The disadvantage, unfortunately, is related to the advantage. Because the stocks are so volatile and the financial reporting relatively more haphazard, many times, even the most well-thought-out plays don't have the desired result. You make money with penny stocks by continuing to make smart plays over a period of time and taking your losses with your wins.

When The Penny Stock Doesn't Have Earnings

Sometimes, what makes a penny stock a penny stock is the fact that its earnings are minimal or non-existent. The stock could be taken to market well before the company posts a profit. When this happens, the P/E ratio is, of course, meaningless because you have a zero in your denominator. Other ratios, such as the price-to-sales ratio and the price-to-cash-flow ratio, are incredibly important for these penny stocks. These ratios can be calculated in the same way as the price-to-earnings ratio: simply replace sales or cash flow data for earnings data. A good benchmark for a strong penny stock is when its share price is half the value of its per share sales value. The cash flow metric is important to study if the company's earnings are questionable. Compare the price-to-cash-flow and price-to-sales ratios for the company over several reporting periods to determine if they look coherent and are indicative of a healthy company. Then, if the price is right, buy!

Where to Find All These Ratios?

The ratios you use to evaluate penny stocks usually come directly from the exchange and are provided by your broker dealer. As was detailed in Chapter 3 of this book, depending on the exchange, certain reporting practices are mandatory for companies that wish to have their stock traded on the exchange.

| 5 |

Winning Companies Issue Winning Stocks

At the heart of all of the metrics and ratios discussed in the previous chapter is the search for a good company. As a penny stock investor, all you're really looking for at the end of the day is a business that knows what it's doing and just so happens to have cheap stock at the moment. You're looking for a company that's having success serving a market, that's able to grow, and is run by competent people.

Look for Companies with Financial Competence

Wow, that's a mouthful, even though the concept is rather simple.

> # a great story + good financials = investment potential

The previous chapter listed a multitude of metrics that can help shed light on a business's ability to attain the financial goals it needs to attain, but if you're looking to invest in a company that's going to succeed big, then you have to make sure that the business itself is clearly viable, that it has a great angle. This type of information about a business can be found in press releases, internet chat rooms, on the company's website, and in the media. Here's a fictional account of what your research process may resemble.

You get a tip in a chat room or on a penny stock investor website that a certain stock trading at $5 per share has great potential. Let's call the stock Wellness Express (WEX). According to your source, Wellness Express was set up in the United States to open a string of healthy, quick-service restaurants in small-to-medium-sized towns. They offer a selection of pre-prepared healthy dishes as well as a made-to-order menu to deliver healthy and fast meal options to their patrons. Their angle is that people will choose to pursue healthy eating options on-the-go when those options are presented to them in a convenient way, and they are more comfortable getting food in a small store environment than they are in a large supermarket where they face a busy parking lot, potentially heavy foot traffic, a long checkout line and limited sit-down space.

The concept resonates with you as a reasonable business angle, so you jump on your broker's website or the website for the exchange where WEX is being traded and check out its numbers. WEX has a quick ratio of 1.3 and an operating cash flow ratio of .8, which is not bad from a liquidity standpoint. The company is making sales at $11.5 for every share; that's a price-to-sales ratio of 11.5 to 5, indicative of a company that's reaching its market. The price-to-book ratio is just above 1, so you know that the current stock price of $5 is cheap. Maybe you've found your diamond for the day, so you buy.

Since there are tens of thousands of penny stocks from which to choose, you can't crunch the numbers for all of them.

> *Note : Some software programs allow you to filter penny stocks by various markets, ratios, and prices. So, if you want to look at a list of all stocks selling at less than $4 per share, with a price-to-book ratio of at least 1, and a quick ratio of 1 or higher, then you can set those parameters in your software and generate a list.*

You have to be able to supplement your quantitative analysis with a qualitative one. You can do this by inspecting the company's image. Has it put any work toward branding? With the fictitious health foods company, WEX, it would be worth a look at the company website and the menu. You could also use Google Maps to take a street-view look at where the restaurants are being placed. Does the area look well-trafficked? Do the sign and façade of the restaurant look attractive? Is the restaurant logo and color scheme attractive?

Branding is especially important with penny stock companies because they are usually in the process of introducing themselves to the market and making a case as to why they deserve market share. In the case of WEX, the company is trying to persuade the market that it's possible to eat healthy on-the-go. Customers must therefore see Wellness Express as a credible source of good food.

Here are some ways for an investor to tell when a company is leveraging good branding toward the promotion of a good business:

- *The company provides value at every interaction point.*
A company that's well branded and destined to survive and thrive aggressively delivers value to the consumer at every opportunity. When you go to the company's website, the company should be making the most of this interaction opportunity, offering to add the customer to a mailing list for special promotions, making its menu easily accessible, providing clear directions to its store or giving the customer the ability to quickly locate stores nearby. These may all seem like common sense concerns, but if a company has invested in creating and hosting a website, then it should be maximizing its utility with every customer visit.

- *The company stands out from the crowd.*
A company destined to succeed must have a sense of inspiration about it. It must be distinct from the other retailers in its space. In the case of WEX, the company defines itself as a fast food alternative: get the speed and convenience of fast food without the nutritional drawbacks.

- *The company cultivates focus in its branding.*

A company that's going to thrive in its market must be clearly focused on its mission and dedicated to serving a specific market sector. One thing that often leads smaller companies to fail or stagnate is over-diversifying or switching course too frequently. If WEX purports itself to deliver healthy food fast, then it doesn't also offer authentic Chinese food, or the best coffee in town, or even the best tasting veggie burger on the market. In reality, there's no reason that WEX can't offer all of these things. In fact, it would be great if it did. But when it comes to the branding of the company, it must remain steady and focused on one particular market entry point.

- *The company communicates well.*

When a company is eager to communicate with its customers via emails, surveys, focus groups or the like, and also communicates with its investors via reports or press releases, then the company is clearly committed to its own success. And that's an important commitment, seeing as not all companies you encounter, especially in the penny stock trade, are going to maintain their passion. Look for companies that aggressively seek feedback and new insight into the market they're trying to reach.

- *The company cultivates its own distinct and consistent style.*

A company that's poised to grow is a company with a very clear and consistent vision for itself. This is perhaps the most important qualitative attribute that you can look for in a winning investment but perhaps also the most difficult attribute to put into words. A company often comes into its own long before it financially matures. This is that rare, elusive point at which the savviest investors have a real opportunity to reap dramatically high returns on a penny stock investment. The key is consistency in branding. Look for evidence that the company has secured a kind of essential image for itself that creates sparks of imminence and inevitability. These abstract elements can be made manifest in a variety of ways. In our WEX example, perhaps the investor notices a rich consistency of branding across the company's in-store experience, its online branding, and its email marketing styles: the same colors, the same voice, the same feel, a sense of a new entity being born and to great purpose. This is where investing, penny stock or otherwise, becomes much more art than science.

The Penny Stock Branding Advantage

One advantage that a smaller, lesser-known or unknown company has over a larger, established company is the ability to flexibly position its brand. Keeping with the example, let's say that Whole Foods saw the need for a healthy meal-on-the-go option in medium-sized cities. Because it already has a reputation for being a higher-end grocery store, it would face an uphill branding battle if it tried to compete with the smaller, newer Wellness Express. Why? Because Wellness Express has cultivated focus around its branding. Wellness Express is about one thing and one thing only: providing diners with great healthy food. Not to say that Whole Foods couldn't eventually position itself to be a viable option for this market need, but it would require a lot more effort on the part of Whole Foods. It would have to readjust its floor plan a bit to allow for an expansion of its dining area and it would need to open a separate checkout station so that diners would be able to check out quickly and eat while their food was still hot. Speaking of hot food, extra care would have to be taken with the preparation and sale of hot food items since more of these items would be consumed on site, rather than taken home where they could be reheated and microwaved.

> *Note : Whole Foods currently allows dine-in customers access to a microwave, which is fine as an added convenience, but if you're really in it to win it in the sit-down game, then you're not directing your customers to use the microwave. Your food will need to be served ready-to-eat.*

All of these alterations to the Whole Food brand would impact other areas of the company's operations. Budgets would be cut, new employees would be hired from different market sectors. New vendor relationships would need to be established, and after it's all said and done, Whole Foods would be faced with the prospect of competition from WEX and any other similar start-ups, copy-cats, and new players. Is it really worth it? For WEX, it is worth it. All it has to do to ensure success is keep its brand focused and on message.

Perform Technical & Fundamental Analyses

Fundamental analysis and *technical analysis* are two terms that get thrown around a lot in the investment world. Fundamental analysis refers to drilling down on the essentials that make a company tick. Who sits on the board of directors, who's managing the company, what is communicated by the company's press releases, and how does this company fare within its industry? Technical analysis refers to looking at all the charts and graphs and other goodies showing how the stock's price has changed over time, its trading volume, and other factoids that may give an indication of what the company's future share value will look like. The methods you use largely depend on the type of investor you are—some call this your "investor personality" – and whether you feel more comfortable betting on trends and data or solid people and a good story.

The Typical Penny Stock

One possible problem with the WEX (Wellness Express) example is that we're envisioning a penny stock that, presumably, already has an active retail location and is generating a substantial cash flow. As a penny stock investor, you're more likely to be confronted with companies that are still in the early research and development phases, approaching some untested market with a new concept, and no one knows whether or not it's going to work. You'll also find everything in between. You'll have a lot of options to choose from, so you'll need to whittle down your choices some.

Here's how you do it:

- **Trade in market sectors that you know.**

Being a successful penny stock investor requires a lot of dedicated research time. It's not always fun. Focusing on market sectors in which you're genuinely interested makes it easier for you to stay up-to-date and intrigued. By becoming the expert in your own field and investing in companies and sectors you understand, you'll set yourself apart from the vast majority of investors who follow the media buzz and move with the swarm from sector to sector, chasing whatever the pundits happen to say is "hot" at the time.

Note: The prices of these media-hyped stocks tend to over-inflate and then plummet, and many investors suffer losses. Many stock "experts" print off weekly tip sheets purportedly telling you where to find the hottest penny stocks. More often than not, the hype results in the stock trading for more money than it's really worth. Its poor fundamentals eventually betray it, and it again plummets in value. So how do you weather the waves of hype? Simple. Learn how to conduct sound fundamental and technical analyses of the stocks you're interested in purchasing.

- **Look for critical pre-market success indicators.**

Depending on the industry, various fundamental factors determine how strong a stock is before its product or service even goes to market. For example, if the company is based on producing and marketing a new invention, then you should check to see that the company has acquired a 10-year patent on the invention. If they haven't received their patent yet, check to see if they're working on improving their product to a point at which patenting is possible. If the company is a bank, a consultancy, or a research group, then inspect the existing and pending relationships. Does the company have financing from a solid source? Does it have sufficient financing to stay afloat for at least 12 more months? Does it have the right partners in place to meet its marketing needs? Advertisers? Agents? Is there any government involvement in the company? Has the company applied for a grant or entered into a dialog with a government entity regarding the future purchase of the company's products? Did it get little more than token attention from these entities, or did it really captivate them?

- *Make sure the company's debt is serviceable.*

It's not uncommon for penny stocks to have debts that exceed their assets. Nonetheless, if the company has incurred debt that's over three times the value of its assets, then it's in a very vulnerable financial position.

How & When to Cash In

Penny stocks investment is quite different from traditional stock investment largely because of all the strange but potent hype that surrounds them. Because the stock price is so volatile, a little bit of good press can send the price soaring. These media pumps don't always work, and the high price rarely sustains itself before going back down. Winning penny stock investors do not buy in the heat of a price-spiking media parade, but are already holding significant shares of the stock at the time the media parade commences.

When you find yourself holding a penny stock that's spiking high, the prudent thing to do is usually to sell within one hour (and no longer than 3 months) after the initial spike. The reason is that in most cases the stock eventually falls back down. Use the cash you free up to reinvest in other stocks. (Remember, the more you invest, the more experience you gain, and the better your insight and intuition become.) If your exploding penny stock continues to climb higher and higher after you sell, don't fret about it. It happens. You did the right thing by insulating yourself from undue risk.

| 6 |

How To Become a Penny Stock Pro

As you've probably gathered by reading this book and digesting what it's offered thus far, there is a wide, perhaps limitless, array of critical factors at play when investing in penny stocks. Learning how to do it right is almost like learning how to dance. There's only so much you can read and watch before you have to just jump in and get started. A lot of would-be penny stock investors are unwilling to risk their already limited supply of money before they feel competent with their investing strategies. Here are a few options to help develop confidence.

Go Virtual

For the beginning investor, **paper trading**, also known as **virtual trading**, is a fantastic exercise to help get the feet wet. You can use a brokerage service (many offer no money or practice trading), or you can simply use pencil and paper to keep track of your virtual portfolio's performance. Peter Leeds, author of *Penny Stocks for Dummies*, claims that simpler is better when it comes to paper trading, "You don't need any fancy software or a complicated spreadsheet. The simpler you make paper trading, the fewer mistakes you'll make—and the easier it will be for you to develop a superior trading strategy.[9]"

When paper trading, it's ok to start off with more "imaginary" money than you'd use were you using real money. Using more money allows you to make more trades and rack up more valuable experience in the market. Ultimately your goal is simply to gain more money than you lose. This goal won't change when you begin to use real money.

---

[9] Leeds, Peter. Penny Stocks for Dummies. Hoboken, NJ, John Wiley and Sons, Inc. 2013.

For the best results, narrow down your industry. Choose a few industries that interest you: tech, health care, entertainment and try to limit your trades to these industries. This focused industry expertise pays off once you begin to notice how the penny stocks in this industry are prone to behaving.

You'll also need to get a few technical details in place, such as the amount of imaginary money that's going to be paid out to your imaginary broker for commissions. Ten percent is a decent standard. You may also want to consider a specific trading period, such as three months, six months, or even a year, after which you will compare the value of your current and your opening portfolio. Setting up a trading ledger isn't very difficult. Just keep it simple, with a column for the date, the company that was bought or sold, the market where you bought or sold, the share price for the transaction, and the loss or profit.

Fg. 13

date	company	market	share price	profit/loss
3/30/16	WEX	OTCQB	$ 3.60	$ 70.00
2/15/16	GBR	OTCPink	$ 1.60	$ (95.00)
2/2/16	TCC	NYSE	$ 4.10	$ 45.00

To keep your penny stock paper trading experience realistic, don't invest all of your money at once, but keep some cash on hand in case new opportunities come down the pipes. Also, you should set goals for yourself that are realistic, similar to the types of goals you would set for yourself were you using actual money. For example, set a goal for 20% growth in your portfolio at the end of 9 months.

Become a Buzz Media Hermit

When you get a tip sheet in your email promoting this, that, and the other "exciting new company," don't read the blurb about the company, but go straight to the disclaimer at the bottom of the tip sheet. Companies often pay people to promote their stocks in an effort to raise funds. When someone is being paid to promote a company, he or she is not delivering an objective analysis as to whether or not a stock is a good buy at its current price.

Incidentally, this same discretion should be applied when evaluating the press releases and statements made by company executives. Remember, they are trying to stay in business and need to raise money in order to do so. Like brokers, company executives are in the business of selling stock. Only pay attention to the material in press releases that offers clear and concrete data about a company's financial wellbeing or some other form of tangible progress, such as securing a patent, opening up a new location, or hiring new staff.

You should be equally skeptical of any sounds-too-good-to-be-true success stories involving a penny stock that shot up in value and made someone a millionaire overnight. People get into penny stock investing because they are interested in seeing big returns, 20 or 30 percent in a few days. In reality, it's much easier to lose money in penny stocks, and unless you're prepared to risk significant sums of cash, you won't become an overnight millionaire.

Of course, there will be good times when you find yourself the benefactor of a serious penny stock upswing. The most important advice you can heed in that moment is to sell and sell soon. You may notice that advice on "when to sell" is conspicuously absent from all of the penny stock newsletters, though the answer is simple. If your stock spikes, sell it as fast as you can. With penny stocks, buyers aren't always going to be readily abundant. One way to improve your ability to sell when you want is to only buy penny stocks that trade in high volume, 100,000 shares a day or more.

How Much Time Should Go Into Research?

The conventional wisdom of investing is that the more research you put into an investment decision, the better your investment will fare. The reality of the situation is that an investor who spends 12 hours researching a single trade can fare just as well or poorly as an investor who spends 2 hours on research. When considering how much time to devote to research, you should consider how familiar you are with the industry in which you're investing. That much is obvious. Perhaps less obvious, but equally as helpful, is cultivating a sense of self-awareness. Understand your investment personality. What inspires you to feel comfortable making a trade? Are you aggressive, or do you like to play it safe? Do you like to be reasonably sure that all your trades are going to make money, or will you invest just for the educational opportunity? If you're very much a type-A personality, then consider instituting a research checklist or research time frame. The checklist ensures that you write down and consider various metrics that are relevant to your investment, while the time frame ensures that the investment decision receives an adequate amount of attention. If you're successful in getting through your checklist and you still have ample time to spare, then learn about some new ratios, or new approaches to fundamental analysis that will make you a stronger investor.

Leeds recommends that you "keep doing your research until you get to the point where you would only blame yourself if the investment didn't do well.[10]" Leeds also recommends immediately ceasing all research into a company as soon as any factors emerge that rule out your purchase, as research can be incredibly time-intensive and there's no sense beating the proverbial dead horse.

---

[10] Leeds, Peter. Penny Stocks for Dummies. Hoboken, NJ, John Wiley and Sons, Inc. 2013.

Screening

Penny stocks are plentiful, and no investor goes through all of the available listings A-Z and researches each stock. You must have some summary-level criteria to narrow your search. These big-bucket categories include:

The Country Where the Stock Issuing Company is Located

One very common criterion for investors is the country in which the stock issuing company operates. Most exchanges and brokerage sites allow you to view where the stock originates, so if you have political or economic reservations, then you know not to research any further.

The "Class Level" Assigned to the Shares

Some companies have tiered classes of shares: normal stock, preferred stock, Class A, Class B. Often these shares confer unique privileges to their owners, such as voting rights within the company. If you don't see yourself voting on the board any time soon, then consider foregoing the extra expense that comes with certain classes of shares. Why pay for what you're not going to use?

Questionable Identities

Knowing that so many investors (bad investors) pour over the pink sheets and throw money at penny stocks randomly hoping to realize some monumental 48-hour return, there's a bit of a niche market out there for bogus stock, stock whose company is really not a serious company, but a fly-by-night operation (if that) looking for an easy way to get money. If the name of a company is exceptionally generic, nonsensical, or if there's no online record of the company when there really should be, then you should probably pass.

Holding Companies

You will certainly come across a multitude of penny stocks with the appendage "Holdings" or "Holding Companies" attached to their names. These companies are created for the purpose of buying and possessing shares of other companies and keeping them under the same umbrella, generally for tax purposes. They are, effectively, legal protection entities, and it's difficult to apply a comprehensive fundamental analysis to them. Many penny stock investors simplify their portfolio by choosing to stay away.

Industries

While many investors prefer to narrow their stock searches by industry-type, they also tend to become frustrated when they discover how difficult it is to electronically sort penny stocks according to industry. Investors often have to do this type of screening manually to ensure that they don't get involved in an industry in which they're not comfortable investing.

Note : According to the Motley Fool,[11] beginning investors should consider choosing industries that are relatively stable, such as basic consumer goods (soap, toilet paper) and utilities. These types of industries offer products and services that will always be in demand even in times of economic downturn. Penny stocks, however, are a bit of a different animal, seeing as the companies can be so small that the threat of bankruptcy is always present.

Know What You Don't Know

There are several immediately relevant factors that may be screen-worthy but are not accessible on-face. For example, you may prefer to only invest in companies that are developing a new service with very few competitors in the market. If that's the case, then you can't execute any sort of automated screening process to filter out the

---

[11] http://www.fool.com/investing/general/2013/05/30/an-easy-investment-strategy-for-beginners.aspx

companies in competitive markets. You have to complete this phase of the legwork on your own.

You may want to stay alert to any significant legal entanglements that affect one of your desired companies. Legal issues can drain cash flows, lead to bankruptcy, and otherwise fundamentally alter a company's ability to function. You can't screen out companies that are legally embattled without direct, manual attention. The investor must also be personally knowledgeable of industry growth or decline, along with other clearly relevant trends likely to influence the price of a stock. Other unscreenable but highly relevant investment factors include pending patents and copyrights. And, finally, most automated screeners cannot parse out the better company managers from the poorer ones, a very important investment criterion that is also left to the investor's personal efforts.

Fg. 14

Healthy Companies	vs.	Ailing Companies
• New hiring and new branches • Compelling story/ business concept • Leaders have a good track record • Aggressively maximizes all available opportunities		• Layoffs and closing branches • Untimely or abrupt turnover in leadership • Unserviceable debt • Poorly conceived concept with no signs of adaptability available opportunities

The Smart Penny Stock Investor "Scales In"

There's undoubtedly something that changes about an investor once she's completed her purchase and is committed to a stock. She's an owner now. She's more inclined to watch over that stock as if it were one of her own children, and perhaps her children's futures do hang in the balance.

Scaling in refers to the technique of buying into a stock (after you've researched it of course) in small increments. While you may lose out if the stock swings wildly upward, adopting this gradual approach gives you an opportunity to ride with the stock for a while as a passenger, observe how it operates and to what, if any, market forces it responds.

It's the hallmark of a novice investor to buy and sell clumps of penny stock all at once without giving himself a chance to experience the stock as an investor before making a significant investment. If you only have a modest investment initially, let's say $250 of an investment that you hope will eventually be $1000, then you may discover something about the stock that you hadn't anticipated. Perhaps the stock is destined to fall in price. At that point, you'll have saved the remaining $750 of your planned investment from losses, *and*, depending on your interpretation of events, you may want to go ahead and scale in another $250 or $500 at this new, lower price. In other words, maybe there's still no reason to believe that your fundamental analysis of the stock's strength was inaccurate, and now you've got your investment secured at a lower price.

Scaling also gives you the ability to incorporate a longer stretch of time into your decision-making process rather than researching, deciding, and investing everything. You research, decide, invest, watch, research, decide, and modify your investment. With this latter approach, you're more likely to put yourself in touch with more meaningful data about the stock and make better decisions overall.

Finding & Calling an Investor Relations Contact

So many penny stock investors don't take advantage of this very basic resource. Almost every penny stock available on the market has a designated person within the company who is in charge of investor relations—even if this person wears a multitude of other hats in the meantime. Successful penny stock investors always seek out and contact a company's investor relations officer before investing.

Before making contact with the company, you should have a somewhat clear idea of what you're going to ask. Don't just call and say, "Tell me about your company and why I should invest." You're not looking for a sales pitch. You're looking for information relevant to your investment. Perhaps you'd like to know if they expect their incoming revenue to increase or shrink over the next year and why. You may also want to know if they plan on hiring more people and for which positions.

Another interesting way to size up an investment opportunity is by contacting a company's competitors. This can be done subtly. You don't have to lie, but it's probably not a good idea to tell the IR (investor relations) officer that you're considering an investment in a competing company. Instead, just say that you're looking to make an investment in that industry and want to ask some questions about the company.

Diversify!

As you're probably coming to understand, penny stocks have a multitude of characteristics that make them distinct from other investments. In other ways, they are just like any other stock market investment and should be treated as such. For example, just as with standard investments—and perhaps slightly more so in penny stocks—it's important to diversify your trades. If you put all of your investment money into one company, then you risk losing everything. Even if you nail the trade and get a nice return on it, if you take your winnings and move onto another stock, investing everything you have, then you're again going to be in a position in which you could lose everything. When the inevitable does happen and you've got all of your investment assets tied up in a penny stock that goes belly-up, the loss will be devastating. This is why you spread your investments out. You must get used to losing a little here and winning a little there, with the ultimate goal of making a larger quantity of winning trades than poorer trades.

Getting the Right Buy at the Right Time

One area in which penny stock investing is quite unique concerns the importance of making well-timed investments. There's always someone with a story to tell you in the world of penny stocks, and the point of the story is always, "Get in now! Before the ship has sailed." Smart penny stock investors take these stories with a grain of salt. The reality of investing in penny stocks is that you're dealing with younger companies, many of which do indeed have big dreams for the future, though few see their goals come to fruition, and *none* of these companies are going to reach their goals ahead of schedule or even on schedule. Penny stock companies always take a lot longer than they think they will to reach their dynamic growth phase. Many investors can become frustrated and discouraged after investing in a "hot" penny stock and watching their money stagnate for months or even years.

Hence, part of the art of penny stock investing is knowing when to invest and when to wait and how to keep watch on a company with the intention of investing later. This distinction is important, because the longer your money sits in a penny stock and waits for the company to find its stride, *the more* risk you assume. Think of a young company as a newborn lemur cub in a jungle full of dangers and predators. Every passing day in the life of a young company is fraught with risk and peril. Threats to the company's survival can manifest at any moment in the form of a lawsuit, a failed patent application, or an emerging, better-funded competitor that takes over the market, not to mention a CEO that decides to throw in the towel. There are a hundred and one ways to lose your money as it sits in a stagnant penny stock. This is why you must learn how to follow a company and watch for the right time to invest. Scale your money into the stock, minimize your risk, while still giving yourself a chance to profit in the event of a big boom!

| 7 |

Technical Analysis of Penny Stocks

If you've got some serious time to spend on penny stocks, then try getting involved with what the experts call technical analysis (TA). TA allows you to determine the validity of the stock and how it will do in the future merely by studying the activity of the trading price of that stock. This requires some in-depth investigation of trading charts and time to learn which indicators are important.

In an earlier chapter, we discussed fundamental analysis - how to learn more about the companies associated with each stock by calling the company's investment liaison, learning about the managers and board of directors, determining how much debt the company has assumed, its exponential growth, and other issues directly related to the company itself. Conversely, with the tools of technical analysis, you don't consider the operations of the company at all. Rather, you look at clues related to trading volume, price spikes and dips, momentum indicators, and similar factors.

Why Use Technical Analysis?

So, if you've done your due diligence as far as fundamental analysis is concerned, why bother with technical analysis? You certainly never have to delve into TA if you prefer not to do so, but most experts actually recommend a combination of the two analyses, as each provides different and important insights into the company and its stock trading action.

In fact, if you're a short-term trader (not really an investor, as we previously discussed), TA requires a lot less patience than fundamental analysis. Watching the charts and gaging trading volume also reveals very accurate buying and selling points. Upward trends, drop-offs in volume – they can be seen quite clearly through TA, and you'll be able to determine with some degree of confidence when it's time to buy or sell.

If you're using technical analysis and trading short-term, you're also minimizing your investment exposure. That means your money is at less risk at any given time. However, it's still important to remember that making purchases and trades based solely on trading charts is – in general – a bit more risky than making decisions based on fundamental analysis. But if you're willing to play the game, you'll be rewarded with some exciting activity.

The Downside of Technical Analysis

TA isn't for everyone, and some of you who are dabbling in penny stocks for the first time might consider these stumbling blocks:

- TA takes a lot of work and time. First you need to learn the ins and outs of reading the charts, then you need to find reliable charts, and – finally – you have to study them regularly, usually daily, if you want to make wise decisions.

- TA has nothing to do with the company whose stock you're purchasing. If you haven't combined some fundamental analysis with your technical analysis, you may miss some important information such as large increases in profits or perhaps sudden growth due to the demise of a competitor. As such, you might miss a good opportunity to either buy or sell.

- If you're making decisions via technical analysis, then chances are you're in it for small gains. That means you may wind up missing larger profits that result when you are an "investor" and are using mostly fundamental analysis and waiting patiently.

- TA doesn't always work with penny stocks, only because the trading volume on many such stocks tends to be quite low. That means patterns are less likely to be established and may be difficult to trust.

If You Want to Use TA

All of that said, if technical analysis is something you'd like to try, here are some tips and suggestions on how to do it and information on aspects of technical analysis that tend to work with penny stocks.

Trading Volume

Penny stock traders can often pick up clues from trading volume. This is simple, pretty straightforward and one of the best indicators of success with a particular stock. Look at the daily trading volume for the last several days (or weeks) and compare it to the volume for the days or weeks before. Is buying and selling activity increasing or decreasing? You'll want to be sure, however, to look for SIGNIFICANT increases or decreases, such as trading that has doubled (on the positive side) or has decreased by more than half (a definite negative). At this point, you may want to try to determine the reasons for the changes, be they good financial reports or something that has scared investors away.

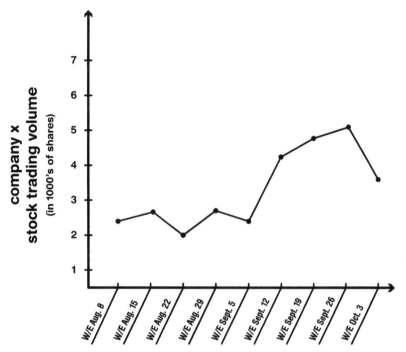

Fg. 15: What happened to Company X in October that caused trading volume to spike?

Support Levels

Look for a stock that has a support level, that is, a price at which shares see an increasing demand that holds the stock at that level. For example, a particular stock may consistently fall towards the $2 mark but then, when it gets close, it heads north again thanks to increased trading.

With penny stocks, support levels tend to form because investors buy at round numbers, like $2 or $3.50. But how do you know if this is truly a support level you're seeing? Leeds suggests that you look for a few different things: 1) increasing trading volume at the support level, and 2) multiple attempts at break down, which means that the more that support level gets tested without failing, the more reliable it is

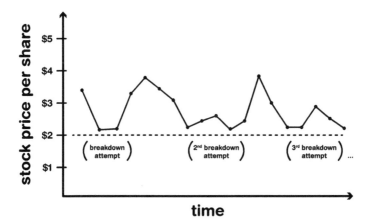

Fg. 16 : The stock depicted in the graph to the left has an apparent support level of appx. $2 that has survived at least two breakdown attempts. If further data can be amassed showing a spike in trading volume as the stock approaches the $2 price point, then the support level is further reified.

Resistance

A resistance level is the opposite of a support level. A stock is said to have a resistance point when it consistently heads towards a particular price – perhaps $3.00 – but never quite makes it there. This is because of increased volume as traders sell their stock when they see that price approaching. This can help you decide when to sell. If you see a stock approaching a ceiling consistently, you can bet that that's the resistance price, and you may want to sell as the stock nears that price and before it falls again.

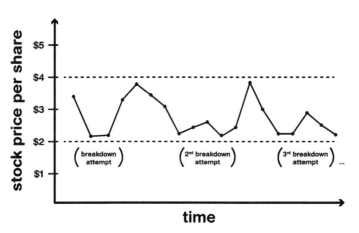

Fg. 17 : The same stock from the previous example appears to have a resistance price of $4. If further data can be amassed showing a spike in trading volume as the stock approaches the $4 price point, then the resistance price is further reified.

Trends

A stock can be on an upward trend, a downward trend, or a sideways trend (stagnant). A trend happens gradually over weeks or months. That means if you were to chart the price per share on a graph using a dot for each day's price, and then connect the dots with lines, you would see either a line going up, a line going down, or a line that stays straight. If you see sudden jumps in those lines – either up or down – that is not a reliable trend.

Price Spikes & Dips

Most experts will tell you not to rely on price spikes as an indicator of when it's time to sell. Because the penny stock market is so much smaller than the standard stock market, a substantial purchase on any given day by one or more buyers can cause a spike. That doesn't mean the price will stay in that position. It could easily fall the next day when trading activity has stopped.

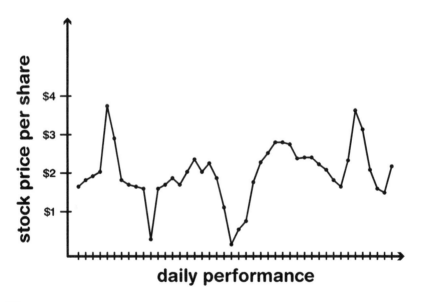

Fg. 18 : Penny stocks are often traded in very low volumes, which can manifest in the appearance of dramatic spikes and dips. A successful penny stock trader must learn to distinguish real trends and meaningful changes from temporary spikes and dips.

The same can be said for dips in price. These often occur because trading volume is low. In other words, the number of sellers of a particular stock far outnumber the interested investors, so the price falls. If you trust that – as with price spikes – the dip won't persist, then it might be a good time to buy. However, you might want to do a little investigation to find out if any detrimental news about the company has been released to the public.

Ceilings

Ceilings occur when a stock realizes a gradual upward trend and then stays at a particular high for a period of time. Also referred to as "topping out", this may be an indicator that it's a good time to cash in and scoop up your profits. Make sure, however, that the upward trend is indeed gradual, perhaps occurring over several months, and look for trading volume to decrease as well, which is probably an indicator that the top price will soon fall. Then sell!

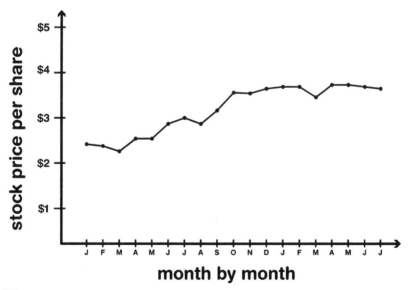

Fg. 19 : The stock depicted in the graph above appears to have a ceiling of appx. $3.50 that's been established over the course of ten months.

Bottoming Out

Whereas stocks can reach a ceiling and stay there for a while before falling, the opposite can happen as well. Look for bottoming out patterns, which are likely to be followed – in many cases – by upward trends. Be sure before you buy that the stock has stayed on a sideways trend for some time. Look for increased trading volume, which indicates that the upturn is about to come. Then buy!

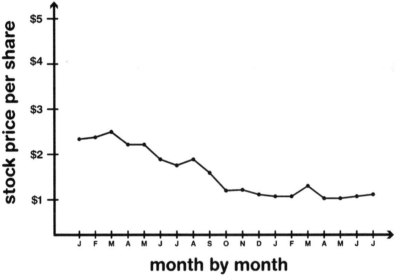

month by month

Fg. 20 : The stock depicted in the graph above is bottoming out at $1. If you can catch a surge in trading volume it means that a lot of people think the price is destined to rise soon!

Momentum Indicators

To gauge a particular stock's momentum – movement in any direction – simply take the current price and compare it to that of a previously selected date. For example, if you want to see the momentum over the last month, simply look for the share price from 30 days ago and compare it to today's price. It's easy to find these indicators on a standard trading chart. These can help you identify new price trends and trend changes or reversals.

Moving Averages

A moving average is simply a calculation of the average price of a stock over a pre-determined length of time in the past. For example, you might want to determine the average price over the last two weeks. You can find this number, of course, by adding up the prices for each day and then dividing that number by the number of days you're investigating. Moving averages can help you spot trends as they begin.

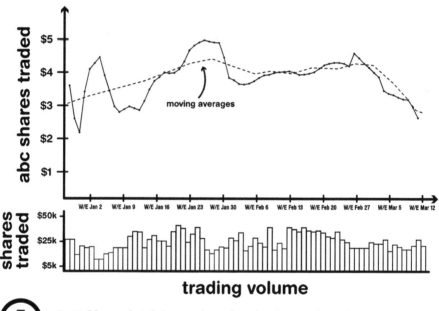

Fg. 21 : Many analytical charts can be configured to show you the moving average for a stock, as well as other factors such as the stock's trading volume.

Relative Strength

Relative strength analyzers look at whether shares of a particular stock are being oversold or overbought. When a stock is oversold – which means that shares are being traded well below what their appropriate value should be – there's a good chance that a price increase is in the near future. Conversely, when stocks are overbought, it means they are being traded at a price well above what the appropriate value should be. Hence, a downward trend is in the air.

This is actually a very simple TA tool and one that has been proven to be often right on the mark. Most charts indicate relative strength, so gaging it takes little or no work.

relative strength index

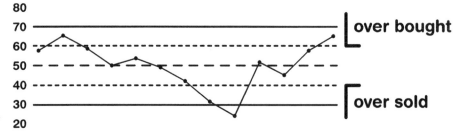

Fg. 22 : The Relative Strength Index can be generated independently or alongside other performance indicators. Usually, the index spans from zero to 100. Index values over 70 are considered overbought and index values under 30 are considered oversold.

| 8 |

Avoiding Scams & Fraud

There's both good news and bad news when it comes to scams in the penny stock market. The bad news is that scams are rampant. The volatility of penny stocks and the laughable reporting standards required (or not required) by some of the shadier OTC markets makes pump and dump, and other scams, irresistible to con artists.

The good news is that there are a few simple rules you can follow to inoculate yourself against the most common and dangerous penny stock scams out there. There are plenty of people who jump into penny stock trading without educating themselves, so scammers have enough available targets, and they don't need to innovate their schemes very much.

Simple Tips

Avoid Buy Lists & Tip Sheets

Because penny stocks are so impressionable, it's impossible to keep fraudulent elements out of the industry. That means "tip sheets," "buy lists," or any publication that specifically chooses and encourages investment in a particular penny stock might not be a good bet. Companies commonly pay penny stock promoters to promote their own stocks, making their analyses very suspect and, at best, highly subjective. Pump and dumpers are usually fly-by-night brokerages that single out or create a bogus penny stock and use their promotion muscle to get the price up. They promote the stock through tip sheets and lists. As a good rule of thumb, never even look at the lists you get in the mail or in your email. Either throw these lists away or just read the disclaimers, which should disclose the relationships the promoters have with the companies being promoted.

Stay Away from the Sketchy Marketplaces

Sure, you can find endless penny stocks on the OTC Pink, but if you want to avoid getting caught up in a stock whose price has been intentionally manipulated by a fraudster, then keep your penny stock trading to better-regulated markets, such as the OTC-BB, OTC-QX, NYSE, AMEX, and NASDAQ. Not only are you less likely to be defrauded while trading in these markets, but you are also supplied with a larger amount of data about the companies in which you're considering investing.

Stay True to Your Strategy & Don't Buy on a Whim

The best defense is a good offense when it comes to avoiding penny stock scams. If you pursue your due diligence, researching companies before you buy them, following them for a while, studying the ratios, scaling your investments, and so forth, then you inevitably make yourself less vulnerable to fraud. You will notice quickly when a stock looks suspect (mainly more expensive than it should be), and you will instinctively repel bad investments.

Don't Give Out Your Personal Information

In the world of penny stock scams, email addresses are instruments of war. Scammers with massive email lists relish in the power of changing a stock price just by pressing send. Their method is simple: secure a huge list of followers, purchase a significant sum of stock, send out an email promoting the stock, and sell the stock when the price artificially goes up. Even if only 3% of an email list's recipients take action and buy the stock, if the email list is big enough and the stock is traded thinly enough, that 3% can alter the stock price. Giving out your email not only supports the underground economy of penny stock fraud, but it is also a recipe for receiving endless spam. Remember, these companies aren't operating above board, and "unsubscribe" isn't in their vocabularies. Worse still, they will gladly sell your email to countless other scammers. To avoid becoming disgusted with the whole penny stock scene, make a point to never give out your email address.

Purchase on Comprehensive Criteria

This tip is similar to tip #3 in that it reiterates the importance of pursuing thorough research on a stock before making the purchase. One way in which investors regularly suffer is by investing in a stock purely on the basis of one or two stand-out factors that are taken way out of context. For example, a company that's doubled its revenue over the last year may entice some penny stock investors to buy right on the spot. But a closer look at the company may reveal that the company had to quadruple its debt in order to affect that doubling of revenue.

Never buy a penny stock on the basis of a story alone. Penny stocks that are attached to amazing stories are often woefully overpriced. Let's say a company is boasting a new type of pet food that uses an ingredient that's been proven to extend the average lifespan of house cats by 15%. The story may sound quite interesting, but what you don't know in the world of penny stocks can always hurt you. Perhaps what you don't know is that 12 other companies are already producing and marketing the same food and the market share is incredibly limited.

The only way to responsibly purchase a penny stock is by researching and following the stock from multiple angles and then scaling in. And after you make your buy-in, it's imperative that you take full responsibility for your purchase.

Why Penny Stocks are Attractive to Scammers

Scammers, like investors, also have criteria they use to determine which stocks to exploit. Penny stocks are generally easier to manipulate than regular stocks because they're so thinly traded that the price can change on a dime. Another advantage of penny stocks for scammers is the lack of required permissions to run promotions. Many times, scammers can tell vivid, elaborate stories about a penny stock without the company's permission. (Larger companies with more to lose would likely take action against a brokerage that engaged in material fabrications to encourage the purchase of its stock.)

Another highly exploitable factor for scammers is the sheer number of penny stocks on the market. Scammers will never run out of new stocks to target, manipulate, lie about, and profit from. If the SEC or the company being promoted gets a whiff of a scam, then the scammers just move on to a different stock. Because most of them make every effort to stay anonymous, they can easily re-target new stocks and even re-brand themselves at the drop of a hat.

But perhaps the number one factor that draws scam artists to penny stocks like moths to the flame is the fact that penny stocks are so thinly traded that most any significant purchase of the stock affects their value. Thus, you can create the Holy Grail for all scammers - an inside line on a stock's future performance.

Isn't This All Illegal?

The reality of the situation is that there are simply too many scam operations out there to regulate. The SEC, with only limited resources, cannot go to the trouble of investigating and prosecuting every stock scam in the market. Instead, a balance must be struck between the limited availability of legal remedy and the efforts exerted by consumers to be savvy and to protect themselves from becoming victims of fraud.

| 9 |

Finding Your Way to the Right Help

If it's hard to find good help these days, then it's exceptionally hard to find good help and advice in the world of stock trading, and it's excruciatingly difficult to find good help with penny stock investing. The main problem is that the massive clutter of nonsense and scammers makes finding sound advice like finding a needle in a haystack. This chapter offers up a few tips on how to cut through the noise and locate credible sources of advice as you pursue your fortune in penny stock investing.

Screen Your Advice & Advisors

As Chapter 5 discussed, penny stock investors must have screening criteria. Otherwise the sheer quantity of penny stocks on the market may baffle you; you simply can't research them all. The problem is that there are a lot of voices anxious to give you advice and, unfortunately, not all of them have your best interest at heart. Here are some indicators that you can look for when you're wondering whether a stock advisor, TV personality, broker, or some combination of all of the above has your best interests at heart.

The Media Superstar

Stock experts are often seeking fame and an audience. And while being able to muster up good stock picks can definitely help an expert gain credibility, there are sometime other attributes that factor into whether a stock broker eventually appears on television, such as that person's charisma, sense of humor, and all around personality.

If you want to check a TV personality's actual competency as an investment advisor, investigate her track record. Have the stocks she has recommended performed well over time? Or is she in the position she's in merely because she's sure to draw good ratings?

The Fragile Ego

Some investment advisors hate being wrong and continue to insist that a stock is undervalued for years on end, regardless of the evidence. Spot these personalities and learn how to distinguish between what may actually be sound advice and what's merely the product of the advisor's insistence on his own infallibility.

The Sociopath

There is a particular class of investors, unsettlingly common on the penny stock scene, that doesn't really care at all whether or not the advice they provide is legitimate, profitable, or even based in reality. They believe that stocks exist in an essentially chaotic universe and the only role of the broker is to encourage transactions and collect commissions. These individuals often don't even enjoy their jobs. They are chronically difficult to reach, reluctant to provide information, and quick to pull the authority card, wanting you to trust them for no other reason other than that they're the purported "experts."

Look for a Verifiable Track Record

Brokers, advisors, or other stock experts who are serious about supplying good advice are proud of what they've accomplished for their clients. They want to show you their statistics and proven ability to read the market. In the penny stock world, these brokers and advisors stand out, because it's easy to contact and communicate with them. They don't to hide behind a shadowy brand that changes every year after the company ruins its reputation by giving out bad advice.

You want to see a track record that spans at least a year if not substantially longer. Spend some time to verify that the picks and successes reported are accurate and not just made up. One way to verify the accuracy of an advisor's pick sheet is to follow his picks for a time and then check to make sure that the picks he actually made are the same as those reported on his track record.

> *Note : Even if you can verify that an advisor has been picking winning penny stocks for a significant amount of time, it's important to realize that this does not mean she will continue to have success. Brokers and advisors often go on hot streaks only to completely implode later down the road. Nonetheless, theoretically, you're much better off if you have someone whispering in your ear who actually cares about the performance of her picks.*

Skepticism is good, but at some point, you're going to have to trust someone or you're not going to go anywhere. It's important to be able to distinguish between the two very different archetypes of "bad stock analyst" and "good analyst who's on a bit of a cold streak." At some point, it's just going to come down to trust. You have to trust the person who's helping you invest your money. Your challenge is to cultivate trust with someone based on a series of rational evaluation points, criteria that goes beyond how well a person dresses, his golf score, or his political affiliation.

conclusion

Buckle up. Penny stocks can be a wild ride, full of fast-paced fun and maybe even some fortune. If you see your penny stock investment strategy as merely a gamble, that's fine, just be sure that you head into your investment experience with clear eyes. If you just start throwing money down on stocks that have interesting names or clever stories, then you will lose money over time, making penny stocks very similar to a casino, plenty of fun, but not profitable in the long run.

On the other hand, if your intent is to use penny stocks to sharpen your acumen for real investing, then you've got a very enlightening and educational experience ahead of you. By applying the techniques in this book and giving yourself time to experience and learn, you'll be able to use penny stocks to make affordable investments in promising companies.

You should also consider utilizing technology to assist you in your penny stock investing efforts, particularly your screening efforts. There are several pieces of software on the market that allow investors to filter through stocks based on their exchange, their trade volume, their prices-to-book (or other key ratios), and on their prices. You are also likely to find similar filtering capabilities when utilizing the online catalogs that your online broker supplies.

Be sure to play your cards close to the chest when dealing with specialty penny stock advisors, brokers, and gurus. The scene attracts many less-than-trustworthy characters and barely upstanding organizations. Get advice from consultants who are pure of motive and capable of showing you an honorable record of great picks.

glossary

Book Price-
The value of a company after its assets are used to clear all of its liabilities.
Assets – Liabilities = Book Price

Cash Ratio-
A liquidity ratio that measures a company's cash and marketable securities in relation to its liabilities.

Current Ratio-
A liquidity ratio that measures a company's current assets in relation to its current liabilities.

FINRA-
(The Financial Industry Regulatory Authority) A private corporation that acts as a self-regulating entity for the financial industry.

Fundamental Analysis-
A fundamental analysis of a stock that focuses on the basic business prowess of a company, the strength of its management team, the conditions presented to the business by its industry, its financial position, as well as the state of the overall economy. The objective of the fundamental analysis is to identify a stock's "intrinsic value," what the stock is truly worth regardless of its market price.

Liquidity Ratios-
A key family of ratios used to assess the ability of a company to pay off its short-term debts and obligations.

Market Capitalization Value-
Commonly referred to as "market cap" value, it is a company's share price multiplied by the total volume of outstanding shares.

Market Maker-
A stock broker or dealer who purchases a certain quantity of stock from a company for the purpose of taking it to a market to be traded.

Operating Cash Flow Ratio-
A liquidity ratio that measures a company's operating cash flow in relation to its liabilities.

Over-the-Counter Exchanges-
(OTC Exchanges) Stock exchanges in which penny stocks are often traded that are not subject to the same rigorous reporting requirements as larger, more well-known stock exchanges.

Paper Trading-
A practice investment exercise whereby a would-be investor decides which stocks to buy and sell on paper, tracking his or her progress without investing real money. Another form of paper trading is virtual trading, whereby the investor's portfolio is tracked using computer software.

Penny Stock-
A stock with a very low share price or very low market capitalization value.

Price-to-Book-
A ratio that assesses the value of
a company's stock in relation to
the company's book price (assets
minus liabilities). The price-to-
book is calculated as such:
Share Price/Book Price per share OR
Market Capitalization/Book Price

Price-to-Sales-
A ratio assessing the value of a
company's stock in relation to its sales:
Share price/Sales per share

Pump & Dump-
A common scheme used by brokers and
other stock promoters to exploit the
volatile, highly impressionable value of
penny stocks. The brokerage purchases
the penny stock at a low rate, then
talks up the value of the penny stock
in the media-via newsletter, phone
calls, emails in order to artificially
and temporarily raise the price. The
brokers then push the "hot" and now
overpriced penny stock to consumers.

Quick Ratio-
A liquidity ratio that measures
a company's accounts receivable,
marketable securities, and cash
in relation to its liabilities.

Stock-
A stock is a piece of a company.
Companies sell stock shares to the
general public in order to raise capital

Stock Market-
The stock market is a place – either
physical or virtual – where stocks and
bonds are traded (bought and sold).

Technical Analysis-
A technical analysis of a stock
involves the study of the stock's
statistics, documenting the stock's
price history, its volume, and several
other attributes. These analyses are
used to identify trends that predict
the future performance of a stock.

Virtual Trading-
See "paper trading."

about clydebank

We are a multi-media publishing company that provides reliable, high-quality, and easily accessible information to a global customer base. Developed out of the need for beginner-friendly content that can be accessed across multiple platforms, we deliver unbiased, up-to-date, information through our multiple product offerings.

Through our strategic partnerships with some of the world's largest retailers, we are able to simplify the learning process for customers around the world, providing our readers with an authoritative source of information for the subjects that matter to them. Our end-user focused philosophy puts the satisfaction of our customers at the forefront of our mission. We are committed to creating multi-media products that allow our customers to learn what they want, when they want, and how they want.

ClydeBank Finance is a division of the multimedia-publishing firm ClydeBank Media. ClydeBank Media's goal is to provide affordable, accessible information to a global market through different forms of media such as eBooks, paperback books and audio books. Company divisions are based on subject matter, each consisting of a dedicated team of researchers, writers, editors and designers.

For more information, please visit us at :
www.clydebankmedia.com
or contact *info@clydebankmedia.com*

notes

REMEMBER TO DOWNLOAD YOUR FREE DIGITAL ASSETS!

Visit the URL below to access your free Digital Asset files that are included with the purchase of this book.

☑ Summaries   ☑ White Papers
☑ Cheat Sheets   ☑ Charts & Graphs
☑ Articles   ☑ Reference Materials

DOWNLOAD YOURS HERE:

www.clydebankmedia.com/pennystocks-assets

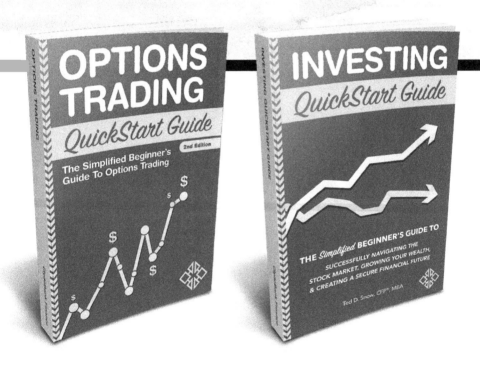

AdoptAClassroom.org

ClydeBank Media is a Proud Sponsor of

AdoptAClassroom.org

AdoptAClassroom.org empowers teachers by providing the classroom supplies and materials needed to help their students learn and succeed. As an award-winning 501(c)(3), AdoptAClassroom.org makes it easy for individual donors and corporate sponsors to donate funds to K-12 classrooms in public, private and charter schools throughout the U.S.

On average, teachers spend $600 of their own money each year to equip their classrooms – 20% of teachers spend more than $1000 annually. Since 1998 AdoptAClassroom.org has raised more than $30 million and benefited more than 4.25 million students. AdoptAClassroom.org holds a 4-star rating from Charity Navigator.

TO LEARN MORE, VISIT ADOPTACLASSROOM.ORG

9 781945 051258